Interactive Notebook: U.S. Constitution

Author: George Lee

Consultants: Schyrlet Cameron and Suzanne Myers

Editor: Mary Dieterich

Proofreader: Margaret Brown

COPYRIGHT © 2018 Mark Twain Media, Inc.

ISBN 978-1-62223-688-6

Printing No. CD-405011

Mark Twain Media, Inc., Publishers
Distributed by Carson-Dellosa Publishing LLC

Table of Contents

Introduction

Why Students Need to Study the U.S. Constitution

For over 200 years, the United States has been guided by the principles set down in the Constitution. The writers made mistakes, some of which have been corrected by amendments to the Constitution and others by a broader interpretation by the courts, but their general principles still stand. It was a most remarkable group of men, and they accomplished one of mankind's greatest achievements. There have been times when individuals have wanted to violate the provisions of the Constitution, but the nation has refused to allow them to ignore the instructions given so long ago during a hot summer in 1787. The style of writing of the Constitution may be troubling at times, but with teacher-directed instruction and the explanations provided in this book, students will be able to understand what the framers of the Constitution meant.

When students become adults, they will have the opportunity to participate in the nation's decision-making process as a citizen, a voter, possibly as a government employee, or perhaps even as an officeholder. How well they understand the principles by which the United States is governed will determine how well they participate as a citizen of this great nation.

Creating and Using an Interactive Notebook

Interactive Notebook: U.S. Constitution is designed to allow students to become active participants in their own learning by creating interactive notebooks. The book lays out an easy-to-follow plan for setting up, creating, and maintaining an interactive notebook about the U.S. Constitution.

An interactive notebook is simply a spiral notebook that students use to store and organize important information. It is a culmination of student work throughout the unit of study. Once completed, the notebook becomes the student's own personalized notebook and a great resource for reviewing and studying for tests.

How the Book Is Organized

There are 15 lessons contained in *Interactive Notebook: U.S. Constitution.* Students will use the **Student Instruction**, **Key Details**, and **Left-hand Pages** to create the left- and right-hand pages of their interactive notebook. Students should have a copy of the Constitution placed in their interactive notebooks to read along with each Key Details page. The italicized text inside brackets on the Key Details page is additional information or an explanation.

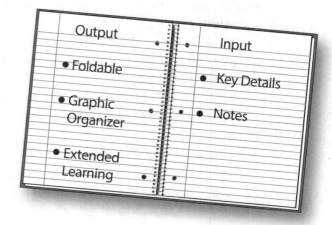

In the copy of the Constitution provided in this book, those parts of the original Constitution that have no modern usage or have been changed by amendments are in italicized type. Capitalization and spelling of words are as found in the original document.

Organizing an Interactive Notebook

What Is an Interactive Notebook?

Does this sound familiar? "I can't find my homework…class notes …study guide." If so, the interactive notebook is a tool students can use to help manage this problem. An interactive notebook is simply a notebook that students use to record, store, and organize their work. The "interactive" aspect of the notebook comes from the fact that students are working with information in various ways as they fill in the notebook. Once completed, the notebook becomes the student's own personalized study guide and a great resource for reviewing information, reinforcing concepts, and studying for tests.

Materials Needed to Create an Interactive Notebook

- Notebook (spiral, composition, or binder with loose-leaf paper)
- Glue stick
- Scissors
- Colored pencils (we do not recommend using markers)
- Tabs

Creating an Interactive Notebook

A good time to introduce the interactive notebook is at the beginning of a new unit of study. Use the following steps to get started.

Step 1: *Notebook Cover*
Students design a cover to reflect the units of study. They should add their names and other important information as directed by the teacher.

Step 2: *Grading Rubric*
Take time to discuss the grading rubric with the students. It is important for each student to understand the expectations for creating the interactive notebook.

Step 3: *Table of Contents*
Students label the first several pages of the notebook "Table of Contents." When completing a new page, they then add its title to the table of contents.

Step 4: *Creating Pages*
The notebook is developed using the dual-page format. The right-hand side is the input page where essential information and notes from readings, lectures, or videos are placed. The left-hand side is the output page reserved for folding activities, charts, graphic organizers, etc. Students number the front and back of each page in the bottom outside corner (odd: LEFT-side; even: RIGHT-side).

Step 5: *Glossary*
Reserve several pages at the back of the notebook where students can create a glossary of domain-specific terms encountered in each lesson.

Step 6: *Pocket*
Students should attach a pocket to the inside of the back cover of the notebook for storage of handouts, returned quizzes, class syllabus, and other items that don't seem to belong on pages of the notebook. This can be an envelope, resealable plastic bag, or students can design their own pocket.

Left-hand and Right-hand Notebook Pages

Interactive notebooks are usually viewed open like a textbook. This allows the student to view the left-hand page and right-hand page at the same time. You have several options for how to format the two pages. Traditionally, the right-hand page is used as the input or the content part of the lesson. The left-hand page is the student output part of the lesson. This is where the students have an opportunity to show what they have learned in a creative and colorful way. (Color helps the brain remember information better.) The notebook image on the right details different types of items and activities that could be included for each page.

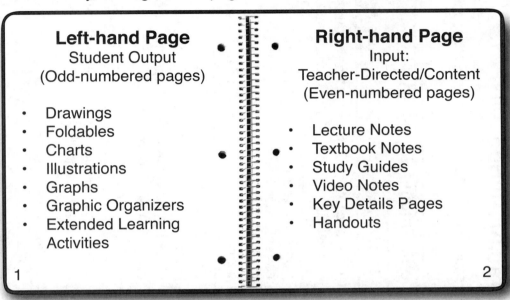

The format of the interactive notebook involves both the right-brain and left-brain hemispheres to help students process information. When creating the pages, start with the left-hand page. First, have students date the page. Students then move to the right-hand page and the teacher-directed part of the lesson. Finally, students use the information they have learned to complete the left-hand page. Below is an example of completed right- and left-hand pages.

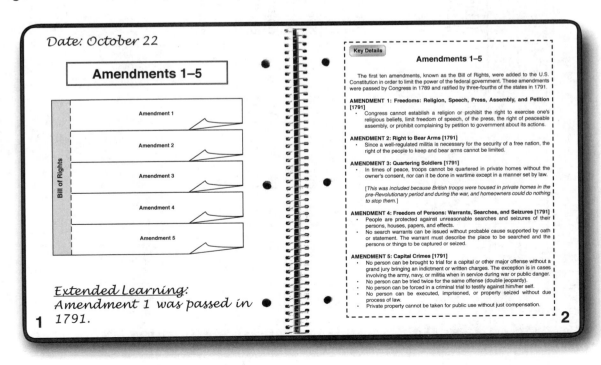

Interactive Notebook Grading Rubric

Directions: Review the criteria for the grading rubric that will be used to score your completed notebook. Place this page in your notebook.

U.S. Constitution Interactive Notebook Grading Rubric

Category	Excellent (4)	Good Work (3)	Needs Improvement (2)	Incomplete (1)
Table of Contents	Table of contents is complete.	Table of contents is mostly complete.	Table of contents is somewhat incomplete.	Attempt was made to include table of contents.
Organization	All notebook pages are in correct order. All are numbered, dated, and titled correctly.	Most pages are in correct order. Most are numbered, dated, and titled correctly.	Some pages are in correct order. Some are numbered, dated, or titled incorrectly.	Few pages are in correct order. Few are numbered, dated, or titled correctly.
Content	All information complete, accurate, and placed in the correct order. All spelling correct.	Most information complete, accurate, and placed in the correct order. Most spelling correct.	Some information complete, accurate, and placed in the correct order. Some spelling errors.	Few pages correctly completed. Many spelling errors.
Appearance	All notebook pages are neat and colorful.	Most notebook pages are neat and colorful.	Some notebook pages are neat and colorful.	Few notebook pages are neat and colorful.

Teacher's Comments:

oh no a turkey

Organization of the Constitution and Amendments

The Constitution is divided into seven articles. Those are divided into sections. The basic format is:

Article I: The legislative branch
Article II: The executive branch
Article III: The judicial branch
Article IV: States
Article V: Amendment process
Article VI: Supremacy of the Constitution
Article VII: Ratification process

Amendments to the Constitution have been added to protect the rights of citizens, expand the numbers of those permitted to vote, allow the government to do something it could not otherwise do, or to improve something in the Constitution.

Amendments 1–10: Collectively known as the Bill of Rights.

Amendment 11: Protected states from outside lawsuits.

Amendment 12: Changed the presidential election process.

Amendments 13–15: Often called the Civil War amendments. They ended slavery, made the former slaves citizens, and allowed African-American men to vote.

Amendment 16: Permitted Congress to collect an income tax.

Amendment 17: Senators were to be elected by the people.

Amendment 18: Prohibited the manufacture or sale of alcohol.

Amendment 19: Permitted women to vote.

Amendment 20: Moved up the date when the president enters office and provided a method for replacing a president who died before taking office.

Amendment 21: Repealed the 18th Amendment.

Amendment 22: Limited a president to 10 years or 2 terms.

Amendment 23: Permitted citizens in the District of Columbia to vote for president.

Amendment 24: Abolished the poll tax that was required in a few states.

Amendment 25: Provided for a vacancy in the presidency and a method of choosing a new vice president after the former vice president became president.

Amendment 26: Allowed 18-year-olds to vote.

Amendment 27: Prohibited Congress from raising its pay until after the next election took place.

Student Instructions: Article I, Sections 1–6

Materials Needed

Glue, scissors, colored pencils

How to Create a Right-hand Interactive Notebook Page

Read the Key Details page. Then cut out the page and attach it to the right-hand page of your interactive notebook. Use what you have learned to create the left-hand page.

How to Create a Left-hand Interactive Notebook Page

Complete the following steps to create the left-hand page of your interactive notebook. Use lots of color.

Step 1: Cut out the title and glue it to the top of the notebook page.

Step 2: Fill in the Houses of Congress chart. Cut out the chart and apply glue to the back. Attach it below the title.

Step 3: Cut out the Sections flap book. Cut on the solid line to create two flaps. Apply glue to the back of the gray tab and attach the flap book at the bottom of the page.

Step 4: Under each flap, write a brief summary of the section.

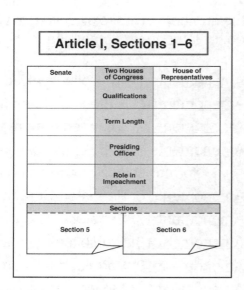

Demonstrate and Reflect on What You Have Learned

Go online and research the number of representatives allocated for each state. How many representatives are allocated for your state? Which state has the most number of representatives? Which state has the least? Write your answers in your interactive notebook.

Key Details

Article I, Sections 1–6

ARTICLE I

The **legislative branch** makes the laws. This branch of the federal government is known as Congress. It is divided into two parts called houses: the House of Representatives and the Senate. Article 1 of the U.S. Constitution describes the powers and responsibilities of Congress.

SECTION 1: Legislative Branch
- The legislative branch consists of a Senate and House of Representatives.

SECTION 2: House of Representatives
- Members of the House are chosen every two years. A representative must be at least 25 years old, a U.S. citizen at least seven years, and a resident in the state where elected.
- The House chooses its own presiding officer (the Speaker) and has the power to impeach.
- The number of representatives per state is based on the size of the state's population, but each state is guaranteed at least one representative.

SECTION 3: Senate
- Each state is entitled to two senators. A senator is elected to a six-year term. A senator must be at least 30 years old, a U.S. citizen at least nine years, and a resident in the state where elected.
- The vice president of the United States presides over the Senate but only votes in case of a tie.
- The Senate tries all impeachment cases. No one can be found guilty unless two-thirds of the senators present vote for conviction. A person found guilty by the Senate is removed from office.

SECTION 4: Elections/Sessions
- States set the times, places, and rules for choosing candidates for Congress unless Congress sets the rules. [*Congress has set the uniform date for elections for the second Tuesday in November.*]
- Congress is to assemble at least once each year.

SECTION 5: Proceedings of Congress
- Each house determines whether a member has been properly elected. Each house sets its own rules and punishes misbehavior. A member may be removed by a two-thirds vote of that house's members.
- Each house must keep a public record of its proceedings.
- Neither house can adjourn for more than three days without the consent of the other house. Sessions have to be held where the other house is located.

SECTION 6: Congress: Compensation and Privileges
- Members of Congress are paid out of the Treasury of the United States. They cannot be tried except for treason, felony, or breach of the peace while Congress is in session. They cannot be a member of Congress and also hold some other office in the federal government.

Article I, Sections 1–6

Senate	Two Houses of Congress	House of Representatives
	Qualifications	
	Term Length	
	Presiding Officer	
	Role in Impeachment	

Sections	
Section 5	Section 6

Student Instructions: Article I, Sections 7–10

Materials Needed

Glue, scissors, colored pencils

How to Create a Right-hand Interactive Notebook Page

Read the Key Details page. Then cut out the box and attach it to the right-hand page of your interactive notebook. Use what you have learned to create the left-hand page.

How to Create a Left-hand Interactive Notebook Page

Complete the following steps to create the left-hand page of your interactive notebook. Use lots of color.

Step 1: Cut out the title and glue it to the top of the notebook page.

Step 2: Cut out the Congress and the States flap chart. Cut on the solid lines to create four flaps. Apply glue to the back of the gray center section and attach the flap chart below the title.

Step 3: Under each flap, write a brief summary of the section.

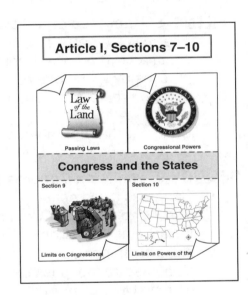

Demonstrate and Reflect on What You Have Learned

Think about what you have learned. Use the information to create a flow chart In your notebook that explains how a bill becomes a law. Use resource books or the Internet if you need help.

Key Details

Article I, Sections 7–10

ARTICLE I (continued)

Article I of the U.S. Constitution describes the powers and responsibilities of the Congress.

SECTION 7: Passing Laws

- All tax bills must start in the House of Representatives, but the Senate may approve or make changes. All other bills may either start in the House of Representatives or the Senate. Both houses of Congress must agree and pass a bill in exactly the same form. The bill is then sent to the president. If the president agrees with the bill, he signs the bill, and it becomes law.
- If the president does not agree with the bill, he can veto the bill by not signing it. Then the bill goes back to Congress. If both houses vote to override the veto, then the bill becomes a law without the president's approval and signature.

SECTION 8: Congressional Powers

- The major powers of Congress include the authority to tax, borrow money, regulate commerce (trade) with foreign nations, establish uniform rules for naturalization (the process by which one can become a United Sates citizen), coin money, establish post offices, create federal courts, declare war, and establish and maintain an army and navy.
- Congress has the authority to make all laws that are necessary for carrying out all powers given by the Constitution to the government of the United States or its officials.

SECTION 9: Limits on Congressional Power

- Congress could not stop the importation of slaves before 1808.
- The Writ of *Habeas Corpus* (right of a person to appear in court) can only be suspended in cases of "Rebellion or Invasion the public Safety may require it."
- No law can be passed that denies a person a trial.
- Congress cannot pass *ex post facto* laws, which punish people for a crime that was not a crime when they did it.
- Congress cannot tax products exported from a state.
- Congress cannot issue titles of nobility.
- No person holding any federal office, "without the Consent of the Congress," can accept any gift, Emolument (profit), Office, or Title, of any kind from "any King, Prince, or foreign State."

SECTION 10: Limits on Powers of the States

- States are denied certain powers, including the authority to make treaties with other countries, coin their own money, have troops or ships of war in time of peace, engage in war, impose taxes on imports, or grant a title of nobility.
- States cannot pass a Bill of Attainder or *ex post facto* laws.

Article I, Sections 7–10

Section 7

Passing Laws

Section 8

Congressional Powers

Congress and the States

Section 9

Limits on Congressional Powers

Section 10

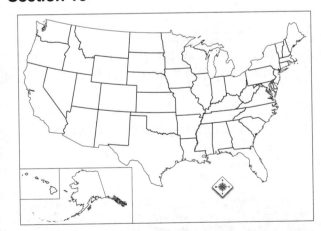

Limits on Powers of the States

Student Instructions: Article II, Sections 1 and 2

Materials Needed

Glue, scissors, colored pencils

How to Create a Right-hand Interactive Notebook Page

Read the Key Details page. Then cut out the box and attach it to the right-hand page of your interactive notebook. Use what you have learned to create the left-hand page.

How to Create a Left-hand Interactive Notebook Page

Complete the following steps to create the left-hand page of your interactive notebook. Use lots of color.

Step 1: Cut out the title and glue it to the top of the notebook page.

Step 2: Fill in each blank on the Executive Branch Flow Chart. Cut out the flow chart and apply glue to the back. Attach the chart below the title.

Step 3: Cut out the two flap pieces. Apply glue to the back of the gray tabs and attach each flap piece to the bottom of the page.

Step 4: Under each flap, write the correct information.

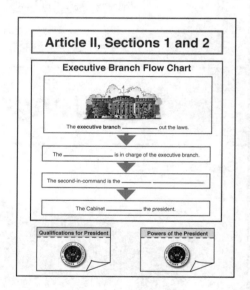

Demonstrate and Reflect on What You Have Learned

Think about the constitutional requirements to be president of the United States. What additional qualifications or life experiences do you think should be added to the list? Write the answer in your interactive notebook.

Key Details

Article II, Sections 1 and 2

ARTICLE II

The **executive branch** of government carries out the laws made by the legislative branch. The head of the executive branch is the president of the United States. The second-in-command is the vice president who supports the president. The heads of executive departments of the federal government, called the Cabinet, advise the president. Article II, Sections 1 and 2 of the U.S. Constitution explains how the two leaders are to be chosen and lists the powers of the president.

SECTION 1: Electing President and Vice President

- The president is in charge of the executive branch and serves a four-year term. The vice president is chosen for the same term.
- The president and vice president are chosen by the Electoral College. The members of the Electoral College are known as electors.
- Each state appoints electors equal to the number of senators and representatives to which the state is entitled in the Congress.

  [*If a state has five representatives and two senators, it is entitled to choose seven electors. In practice, each political party chooses seven electors in case it wins. If Party B's candidate wins the election, Party B's electors cast all seven votes; Party A's electors do not vote.*]

- Congress determines the date for choosing electors, and the day on which they will vote. A uniform voting date has been established (the Tuesday after the first Monday in November).
- To be eligible for the office of president, a person must be a natural-born citizen; must be at least 35 years old; and have lived in the United States for 14 years.
- If the president is unable to discharge the powers and duties of the office, the vice president acts as president until the president is able to resume office. If the president is removed from office, resigns, or dies, the vice president becomes president for the remainder of the term.
- The president is to receive a salary.
- The president takes an oath to faithfully perform the duties of the office of the president and "preserve, protect, and defend the Constitution of the United States."

SECTION 2: Powers Given to the President

- The president is the commander-in-chief of the army and navy of the United States and the militia when called into the service of the United States.
- The president has the power to make treaties, which do not become effective unless two-thirds of the Senate agree.
- The president has the power to nominate ambassadors, justices of the Supreme Court, and judges in other federal courts. They must be approved by the Senate.

Article II, Sections 1 and 2

Executive Branch Flow Chart

The **executive branch** _____ out the laws.

The _____ is in charge of the executive branch.

The second-in-command is the _____ _____.

The Cabinet _____ the president.

Qualifications for President

Powers of the President

Student Instructions: Article II, Sections 3 and 4

Materials Needed

Glue, scissors, colored pencils

How to Create a Right-hand Interactive Notebook Page

Read the Key Details page. Then cut out the page and attach it to the right-hand page of your interactive notebook. Use what you have learned to create the left-hand page.

How to Create a Left-hand Interactive Notebook Page

Complete the following steps to create the left-hand page of your interactive notebook. Use lots of color.

Step 1: Cut out the title and glue it to the top of the notebook page.

Step 2: Cut out the President flap piece. Apply glue to the back of the gray tab and attach the flap piece below the title.

Step 3: Under the flap, list the additional duties and powers of the president.

Step 4: Fill in the blanks on the Impeachment piece. Cut out the piece. Apply glue to the back and attach it at the bottom of the page.

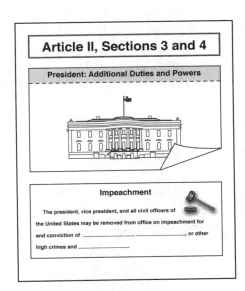

Demonstrate and Reflect on What You Have Learned

As of 2017, only two presidents have had impeachment charges brought by the House of Representatives. Research to find out the names of the two presidents, the charges brought against each, and the final results. Write the answers in your interactive notebook.

Key Details

Article II, Sections 3 and 4

ARTICLE II (continued)

Article II, Section 3 of the U.S. Constitution explains the responsibilities of the president. Section 4 defines the impeachment process.

SECTION 3: Additional Duties and Powers of the President

- From time to time the president gives Congress information on how the nation is doing and recommends policies considered to be needed and useful. [*This is usually done during the State of the Union address in January of each year.*]
- Under unusual circumstances, the president can call Congress, or one of the houses of Congress, into special session.
- If the two houses are in disagreement over the time of adjournment (when they are going to take a break), the president can adjourn them for a certain amount of time.
- The president receives foreign ambassadors and other public officials.
- The president sees that the laws are faithfully executed.
- The president commissions all officers of the United States.

[*Receiving and sending ambassadors is a more important role than many might assume. If the president does not approve of the policies of a certain country and refuses to accept an ambassador from that country, the United States does not have diplomatic relations with them.*]

SECTION 4: Impeachment

- The president, vice president, and all civil officers of the United States can be removed from office on impeachment for and conviction of treason, bribery, or other high crimes and misdemeanors.

[*The process of impeachment and trial is spelled out in Article I of the Constitution. Grounds for impeachment and removal are given in Article II. Treason is an attempt to overthrow your own government or betraying its best interests through dealings with a foreign government. Bribery is receiving money or some valuable gift that influences one's policies. High crimes are violations of law of a serious nature. Misdemeanors are minor crimes.*]

Article II, Sections 3 and 4

President: Additional Duties and Powers

Impeachment

The president, vice president, and all civil officers of

the United States may be removed from office on impeachment for

and conviction of _____, _____, or other

high crimes and _____.

Student Instructions: Article III

Materials Needed

Glue, scissors, colored pencils

How to Create a Right-hand Interactive Notebook Page

Read the Key Details page. Then cut out the page and attach it to the right-hand page of your interactive notebook. Use what you have learned to create the left-hand page.

How to Create a Left-hand Interactive Notebook Page

Complete the following steps to create the left-hand page of your interactive notebook. Use lots of color.

Step 1: Cut out the title and glue it to the top of the notebook page.

Step 2: Cut out the Judicial Branch flap piece. Apply glue to the back of the gray tab and attach it below the title. Under the flap, explain the job of the judicial branch.

Step 3: Cut out the Federal Courts flap piece. Apply glue to the back of the gray tab and attach it below the Judicial Branch flap piece. Under the flap list the types of cases heard in federal courts.

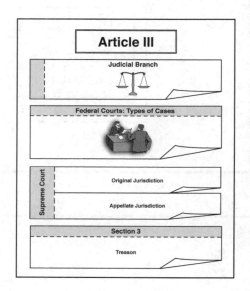

Step 4: Cut out the Supreme Court flap book. Cut on the solid line to create two flaps. Apply glue to the back of the gray tab and attach it below the Federal Courts flap piece. Under the flaps, explain the type of jurisdiction.

Step 5: Cut out the Treason flap piece. Apply glue to the back of the gray tab and attach it at the bottom of the page. Under the flap, summarize Section 3, which explains treason.

Demonstrate and Reflect on What You Have Learned

Go online and locate the names of the current Supreme Court justices. Write their names in your interactive notebook. Circle the name of the Chief Justice.

Key Details

Article III

ARTICLE III

    The **judicial branch** interprets or explains the meaning of laws made by the legislative branch. This branch is made up of the Supreme Court and other federal courts.

SECTION 1: Courts and Compensation of Judges
- Judicial power of the United States is vested in the Supreme Court and other courts that Congress creates.
- Judges in all federal courts receive salaries on a regular basis.

SECTION 2: Jurisdiction and Trial by Jury
- The judicial power of federal courts includes all cases arising under the Constitution and the laws and treaties made by the United States; to all cases involving ambassadors, other public officials, and consuls; to all cases involving naval and maritime supervision; to controversies in which the United States is a party; to controversies between two or more states; cases between citizens of different states; and cases between a state or one of its citizens and foreign governments and their citizens or subjects.
- Original Jurisdiction: In all cases involving ambassadors, other public officials, consuls, and those in which a state is a party, the Supreme Court is the first court to hear the case.
- Appellate Jurisdiction: Cases first tried in other courts can be appealed to the Supreme Court, unless Congress makes different rules.
- Except in cases of impeachment, trials in federal courts will be by jury, and the trial will take place in the state where the crime was committed, but when not committed within a state, the trial can be anywhere that Congress, by some law, has directed.

SECTION 3: Treason
- Treason against the United States is limited to making war against the United States, switching to the enemy side, or aiding or helping the enemy.
- No person can be convicted of treason without two witnesses to the same open or unconcealed action or without confessing to the crime in open court.
- Congress is given the authority to set the punishment for treason, but that punishment cannot include punishment for members of the family who were not involved in the crime.
- Any property seized must be returned to the heirs after the traitor's death.

Article III

Judicial Branch

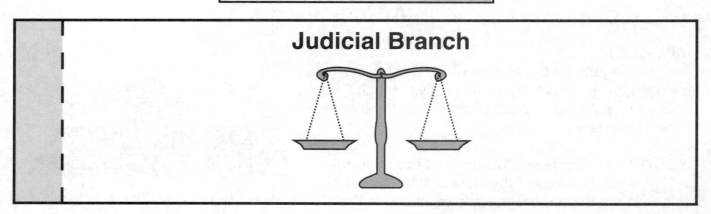

Federal Courts: Types of Cases

Supreme Court

Original Jurisdiction

Appellate Jurisdiction

Section 3

Treason

Student Instructions: Articles IV and V

Materials Needed

Glue, scissors, colored pencils

How to Create a Right-hand Interactive Notebook Page

Read the Key Details page. Then cut out the section and attach it to the right-hand page of your interactive notebook. Use what you have learned to create the left-hand page.

How to Create a Left-hand Interactive Notebook Page

Complete the following steps to create the left-hand page of your interactive notebook. Use lots of color.

Step 1: Cut out the title and glue it to the top of the notebook page.

Step 2: Cut out the Article IV flap book. Cut on the solid lines to create four flaps. Apply glue to the back of the map section and attach the flap book below the title.

Step 3: Under each flap, answer the question.

Step 4: Cut out the Article V flap book. Cut on the solid line to create two flaps. Apply glue to the back of the gray tab and attach the flap book at the bottom of the page.

Step 5: Under each flap, answer the question.

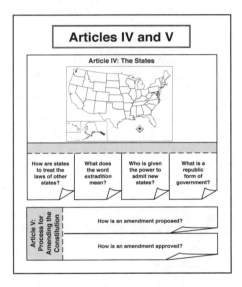

Demonstrate and Reflect on What You Have Learned

Think about what you have learned. Why do you think the framers (writers) of the Constitution provided a way for the document to be amended? Write the answer in your interactive notebook.

Key Details

Articles IV and V

ARTICLE VI
The Constitution established a strong central government. This article explains the relationship of states to one another and the relationship between states and the national government.

SECTION 1: Relationship Between States
- Each state is to give full acceptance of the laws and judicial proceedings of other states. Congress has the authority to develop a process by which this takes place.

SECTION 2: Privileges and Immunities of Citizens
- Citizens of one state are entitled to all the rights of citizens in other states.
- If a person broke a law in one state and is captured in another state, the person is returned to the state where the crime was committed. This is called **extradition**.

SECTION 3: New States/Governing Territories
- New states can be created by Congress, but they cannot be formed by putting two existing states together or taking land away from a state without the consent of the legislature of the state or states and by the approval of Congress.
- Congress has the power to sell or make rules and regulations for the territories or other properties of the United States.

SECTION 4: Federal Protection of the States
- Congress guarantees the states a centralized representative government (republic) that protects them from being invaded
- A governor can request federal protection for the state against rioters.

ARTICLE V
This article explains how the Constitution can be amended or changed. The changes are called **amendments**. Amendments allow a peaceful means of changing the Constitution but are difficult to pass. This keeps popular but bad ideas from becoming part of the Constitution.
- Amendments can be proposed by two methods 1) By a two-thirds vote of both houses of Congress and 2) If two-thirds of state legislatures call for a convention for proposing amendments.
- The proposed amendment must then be approved by three-fourths of state legislatures or by conventions in three-fourths of the states.
- No state, without its permission, can be deprived of equal representation in the Senate.

AMENDMENT XXVIII

Articles IV and V

Article IV: The States

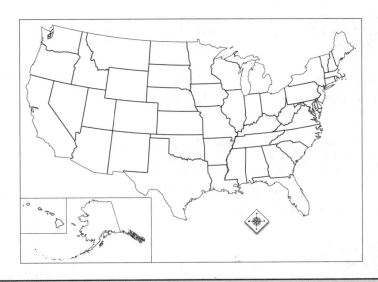

How are states to treat the laws of other states?	What does the word *extradition* mean?	Who is given the power to admit new states?	What is a republic form of government?

Article V: Process for Amending the Constitution

How is an amendment proposed?

How is an amendment approved?

Student Instructions: Articles VI and VII

Materials Needed

Glue, scissors, colored pencils

How to Create a Right-hand Interactive Notebook Page

Read the Key Details page. Then cut out the page and attach it to the right-hand page of your interactive notebook. Use what you have learned to create the left-hand page.

How to Create a Left-hand Interactive Notebook Page

Complete the following steps to create the left-hand page of your interactive notebook. Use lots of color.

Step 1: Cut out the title and glue it to the top of the notebook page.

Step 2: Cut out the Article VI flap book. Cut on the solid lines to create three flaps. Apply glue to the back of the gray tab and attach the flap book below the title.

Step 3: Under each flap, explain the topic.

Step 4: Fill in the blanks on the Article VII piece. Cut out the piece and apply glue to the back. Attach it at the bottom of the page.

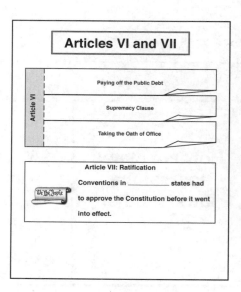

Demonstrate and Reflect on What You Have Learned

Research the oath of office for the president and the oath for all other federal employees. Record both oaths in your interactive notebook.

Articles VI and VII

ARTICLE VI: Constitution as Supreme Law

Article VI establishes that the Constitution and federal laws are the "supreme Law of the Land" and have higher authority than state laws.

- Debts of the United States incurred during the Confederation period are valid responsibilities of the federal government.
- Supremacy Clause: The Constitution and the laws and treaties made by the United States to carry out its provisions are the supreme law of the land. Judges in any state are bound to abide by the provisions of the Constitution in their rulings regardless of any provision in state law that conflicts with it.
- All members of Congress, all members of state legislatures, and all officers of the executive and judicial branches of the federal or state governments are to swear by oath or affirmation to support this Constitution.
- No religious test can ever be required as a qualification for any federal office.

[*The Supremacy Clause in Article VI brought state constitutions, laws, governors, legislators, and all public officials in line to uphold and defend the U.S. Constitution. Despite many differences that still exist in state laws, they all must conform to the Constitution, laws, and treaties of the United States.*]

ARTICLE VII: Ratification

Article VII states the process for ratification (approval) of the Constitution.

- Ratification of the Constitution by conventions in nine states was sufficient for it to go into effect in those approving states.

[*The ratification provision in Article VII faced great difficulty in some states. New York ratified it by a bare majority of 30–27. At the time Washington was inaugurated as the first president, two states were still outside the Union: North Carolina and Rhode Island. When they realized that being outside made business and dealings with other states difficult, if not impossible, they caved in and approved. The main argument used by critics of the Constitution (labeled Anti-Federalists) was that it had no bill of rights. James Madison promised that when Congress assembled, that would be corrected, and it was.*]

Articles IV and V

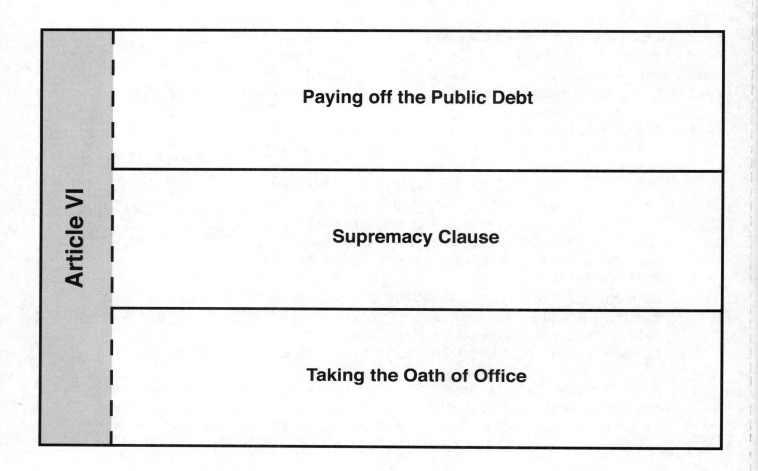

Article VI

Paying off the Public Debt

Supremacy Clause

Taking the Oath of Office

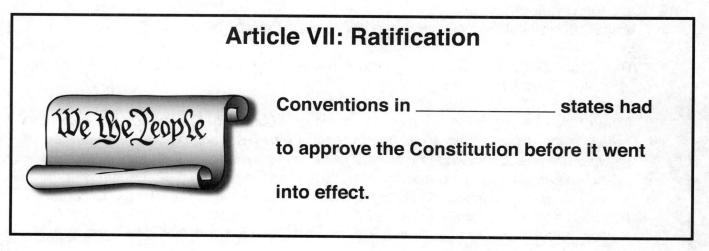

Article VII: Ratification

We The People

Conventions in _____ states had to approve the Constitution before it went into effect.

Student Instructions: Amendments 1–5

Materials Needed

Glue, scissors, colored pencils

How to Create a Right-hand Interactive Notebook Page

Read the Key Details page. Then cut out the page and attach it to the right-hand page of your interactive notebook. Use what you have learned to create the left-hand page.

How to Create a Left-hand Interactive Notebook Page

Complete the following steps to create the left-hand page of your interactive notebook. Use lots of color.

Step 1: Cut out the title and glue it to the top of the notebook page.

Step 2: Cut out the Bill of Rights flap book. Cut on the solid lines to create five flaps. Apply glue to the back of the gray tab and attach the flap book below the title.

Step 3: Under each flap, write a brief summary of the amendment.

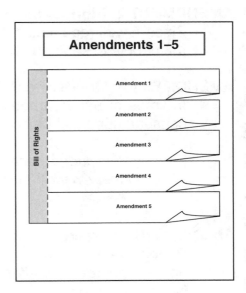

Demonstrate and Reflect on What You Have Learned

In your interactive notebook, draw a symbol for each of the freedoms protected under the first five amendments. Label each drawing with the name of the freedom.

Key Details

Amendments 1–5

The first ten amendments, known as the Bill of Rights, were added to the U.S. Constitution in order to limit the power of the federal government. These amendments were passed by Congress in 1789 and ratified by three-fourths of the states in 1791.

AMENDMENT 1: Freedoms: Religion, Speech, Press, Assembly, and Petition [1791]
- Congress cannot establish a religion or prohibit the right to exercise one's religious beliefs, limit freedom of speech, of the press, the right of peaceable assembly, or prohibit complaining by petition to government about its actions.

AMENDMENT 2: Right to Bear Arms [1791]
- Since a well-regulated militia is necessary for the security of a free nation, the right of the people to keep and bear arms cannot be limited.

AMENDMENT 3: Quartering Soldiers [1791]
- In times of peace, troops cannot be quartered in private homes without the owner's consent, nor can it be done in wartime except in a manner set by law.

 [*This was included because British troops were housed in private homes in the pre-Revolutionary period and during the war, and homeowners could do nothing to stop them.*]

AMENDMENT 4: Freedom of Persons: Warrants, Searches, and Seizures [1791]
- People are protected against unreasonable searches and seizures of their persons, houses, papers, and effects.
- No search warrants can be issued without probable cause supported by oath or statement. The warrant must describe the place to be searched and the persons or things to be captured or seized.

AMENDMENT 5: Capital Crimes [1791]
- No person can be brought to trial for a capital or other major offense without a grand jury bringing an indictment or written charges. The exception is in cases involving the army, navy, or militia when in service during war or public danger.
- No person can be tried twice for the same offense (double jeopardy).
- No person can be forced in a criminal trial to testify against him/her self.
- No person can be executed, imprisoned, or property seized without due process of law.
- Private property cannot be taken for public use without just compensation.

Amendments 1–5

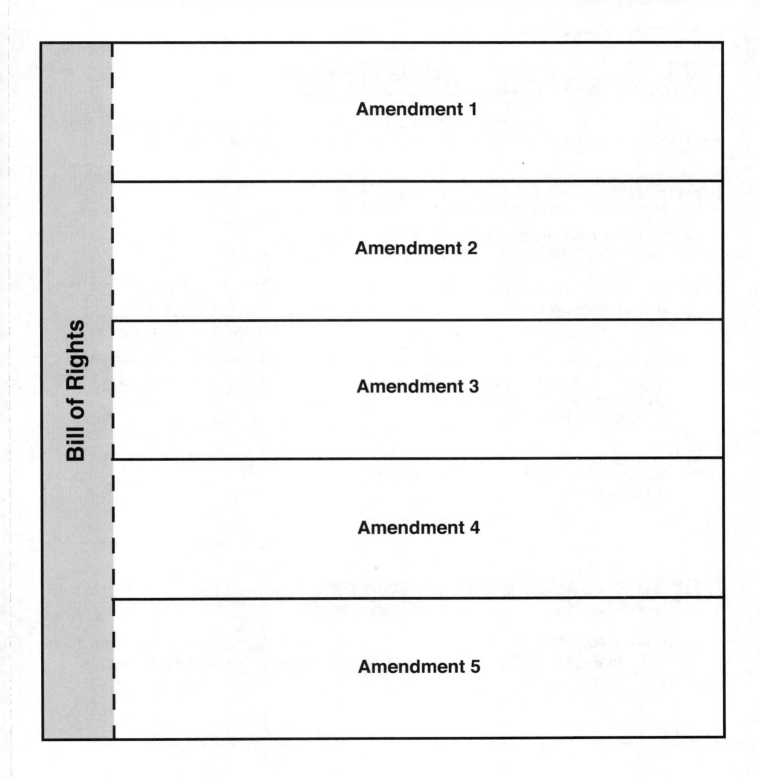

Bill of Rights

Amendment 1

Amendment 2

Amendment 3

Amendment 4

Amendment 5

29

Student Instructions: Amendments 6–10

Materials Needed

Glue, scissors, colored pencils

How to Create a Right-hand Interactive Notebook Page

Read the Key Details page. Then cut out the page and attach it to the right-hand page of your interactive notebook. Use what you have learned to create the left-hand page.

How to Create a Left-hand Interactive Notebook Page

Complete the following steps to create the left-hand page of your interactive notebook. Use lots of color.

Step 1: Cut out the title and glue it to the top of the notebook page.

Step 2: Cut out the Bill of Rights flap book. Cut on the solid lines to create five flaps. Apply glue to the back of the gray tab and attach the flap book below the title.

Step 3: Under each flap, write a brief summary of the amendment.

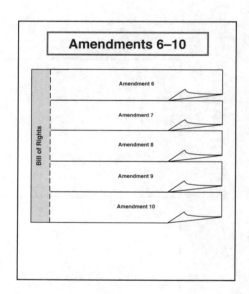

Demonstrate and Reflect on What You Have Learned

Research your state constitution. Does it include a bill of rights? If it does, compare it with the federal Bill of Rights. List the similarities and differences in your interactive notebook.

Key Details

Amendments 6–10

The first ten amendments, known as the Bill of Rights, were added to the U.S. Constitution in order to limit the power of the federal government. These amendments were passed by Congress in 1789 and ratified by three-fourths of the states in 1791.

AMENDMENT 6: Trial by Jury: Accusations, Witnesses, Counsel [1791]
- The accused is entitled to a speedy trial in an open court.
- The accused is to be tried in the state and district where the crime was committed.
- The accused has the right to know the charges made against him/her, to confront the witnesses testifying against him/her, to require testimony from witnesses who can testify for him/her, and to have legal counsel for his/her defense.

AMENDMENT 7: Civil Law [1791]
- In civil suits where the amount disputed is over $20, the parties have a right to trial by jury.
- Any appeal of the jury's ruling must be judged by common law rules.

[*This amendment involves non-criminal situations where the issue is usually damages.*]

AMENDMENT 8: Bails, Fines, and Punishments [1791]
- Excessive bail cannot be required, excessive fines cannot be imposed, and cruel and unusual punishments cannot be inflicted.

[*Bail is a pledge of money or property guaranteeing the accused will appear in court. Torture and slow death are examples of cruel and unusual punishments.*]

AMENDMENT 9: Rights Retained by the People [1791]
- A person may have other rights that might not have been listed in the Constitution.

[*In other words, not every right may have been included, but that does not mean an American has lost them.*]

AMENDMENT 10: Rights Reserved to the States [1791]
- The states and citizens of the states have not lost their rights just because they have not been included.

[*The 9th and 10th Amendments were inserted to make sure the federal government did not take away a freedom just because it was not mentioned.*]

Amendments 6–10

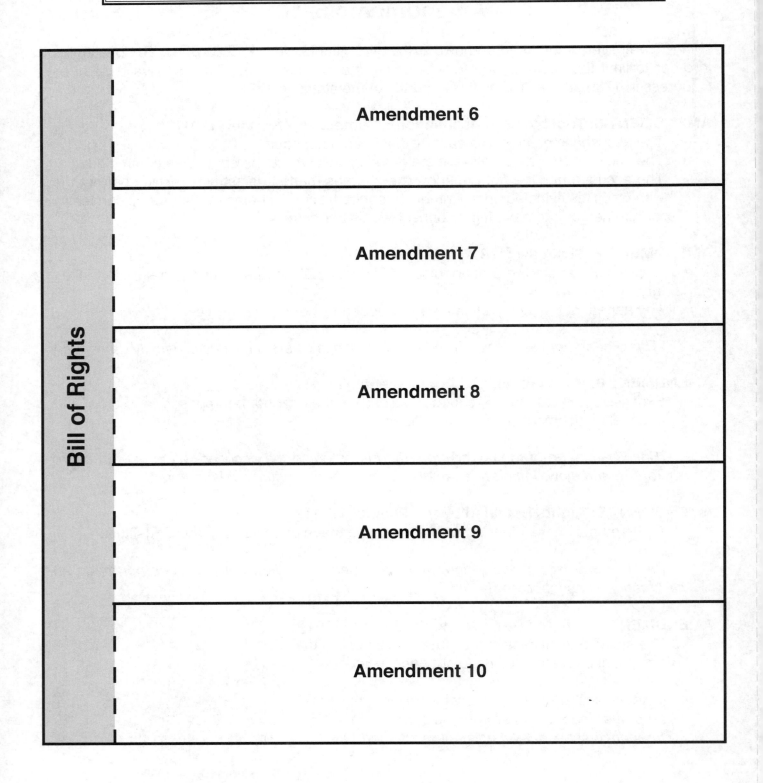

Bill of Rights

Amendment 6

Amendment 7

Amendment 8

Amendment 9

Amendment 10

Student Instructions: Amendments 11 and 12

Materials Needed

Glue, scissors, colored pencils

How to Create a Right-hand Interactive Notebook Page

Read the Key Details page. Then cut out the page and attach it to the right-hand page of your interactive notebook. Use what you have learned to create the left-hand page.

How to Create a Left-hand Interactive Notebook Page

Complete the following steps to create the left-hand page of your interactive notebook. Use lots of color.

Step 1: Cut out the title and glue it to the top of the notebook page.

Step 2: Cut out the two Amendment pockets. Fold back the gray tabs on the dotted lines. Apply glue to the tabs and attach each pocket below the title.

Step 3: Cut apart the sentence strips. Place each strip in the correct pocket.

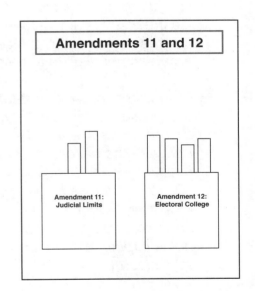

Demonstrate and Reflect on What You Have Learned

Think about what you have learned. In your interactive notebook, list several reasons why the presidential election of 1800 resulted in Amendment 12.

Key Details

Amendments 11 and 12

Before the Civil War, twelve amendments had been ratified: the first ten (the Bill of Rights) to protect individual and state liberties, the eleventh to protect states from being sued, and the twelfth to correct an unexpected defect in the original Constitution.

AMENDMENT 11: Judicial Limits [1798]
- A state cannot be sued by citizens of another state.
- A state cannot be sued by citizens or subjects of foreign countries.

AMENDMENT 12: Electoral College [1804]
- The members of the Electoral College are to cast separate ballots for president and vice president.
- If no candidate for president receives a majority of votes, the House is to choose the president from the top three candidates; each state casts one vote.
- If a president is not chosen by March 4 (Inauguration Day), the vice president is to serve as president until the choice is made. [*Amendment 20 changes the date to January 20.*]
- A person not eligible to be president is not eligible to be vice president.

[*The writers of the Constitution did not have a crystal ball and did not predict the coming of political parties. Under the original Constitution, electors cast two votes (for president and vice president). The candidate with the most votes became president, and the one with the second-highest number became vice president. By 1800, political parties developed, and the candidate for president (Jefferson) had exactly the same number of electoral votes as the vice presidential candidate Burr. Following the procedure required by Article II, Section 1, Clause 3 of the Constitution, the election went to the House where Jefferson was chosen president. Obviously, this situation should not be repeated. This helps explain why Amendment 12 was needed and approved before the next election took place.*]

Amendments 11 and 12

Amendment 11:
Judicial Limits

Amendment 12:
Electoral College

If a president is not chosen by Inauguration Day, the vice president is to serve as president until the choice is made.
A state cannot be sued by citizens of another state.
A person who is not eligible to be president is not eligible to be vice president.
The House of Representatives chooses the president from the top three candidates if no candidate receives a majority of votes.
A state cannot be sued by citizens or subjects of a foreign country.
The Electoral College will vote for president and vice president on separate ballots.

Student Instructions: Amendments 13, 14, and 15

Materials Needed

Glue, scissors, colored pencils

How to Create a Right-hand Interactive Notebook Page

Read the Key Details page. Then cut out the page and attach it to the right-hand page of your interactive notebook. Use what you have learned to create the left-hand page.

How to Create a Left-hand Interactive Notebook Page

Complete the following steps to create the left-hand page of your interactive notebook. Use lots of color.

Step 1: Cut out the title and glue it to the top of the notebook page.

Step 2: Fill in the blanks on the Amendments piece. Cut out the piece and apply glue to the back. Attach it below the title.

Step 3: Cut out the puzzle flaps. Match each amendment with the correct description. Apply glue to the back of the gray tabs and attach the matched puzzle flaps below the title.

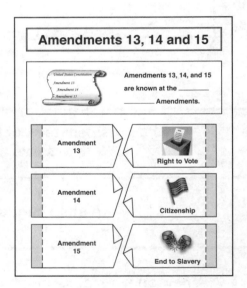

Step 4: Under each set of matched puzzle flaps, write a brief summary of the amendment.

Demonstrate and Reflect on What You Have Learned

Think about what you have learned. How do you think the Civil War Amendments advanced the cause of civil rights? Write your answer in your interactive notebook.

Key Details

Amendments 13, 14, and 15

Amendments 13, 14, and 15 are known as the Civil War Amendments. The 13th Amendment ended slavery. The 14th Amendment settled the issue of citizenship for African Americans, defined citizenship, and ensured the rights of citizens. The 15th Amendment gave voting rights to African Americans.

AMENDMENT 13: Abolition of Slavery [1865]
- Slavery and other forms of involuntary labor, except as punishment for crime, cannot exist in the United States or in any place controlled by the United States.

AMENDMENT 14: Citizenship [1868]
SECTION 1: Due Process of Law
- All persons born or naturalized in the United States and subject to its authority are citizens of the United States and of the state where they reside.
- No state can make or enforce laws that take away the rights and privileges of citizens of the United States.
- No state can take away from any person their life, liberty, or property without fair processes, nor deny equal protection of the law to anyone within its boundaries.

SECTION 2: Apportionment and Right to Vote
- For purposes of representation in the House, everyone in the state counts as a person, except untaxed Native Americans.
  [*The Indian Citizenship Act of 1924 recognized the U.S. citizenship of Native Americans.*]
- If male U.S. citizens over 21 are denied the vote for electors for president and vice president, that state's representation in Congress will be reduced proportionally.

SECTION 3: Penalties for Engaging in Insurrection
- A person who has participated in rebellion or insurrection against the United States cannot hold state or federal offices.
  [*The original intention was to ban leaders of the Confederacy from holding state or federal offices.*]

SECTION 4: Public Debt
- The public debt of the United States, including future debts caused by pensions and bounties during the war, is valid. The Confederate war debt or state debts incurred in fighting the war or claims for loss of emancipated slaves are not valid.

AMENDMENT 15: Right to Vote [1870]
- No citizen can be denied the right to vote because of race, color, or because the person had been a slave.

Amendments 13, 14, and 15

Amendments 13, 14, and 15 are known as the _____ _____ Amendments.

Amendment 13

Right to Vote

Amendment 14

Citizenship

Amendment 15

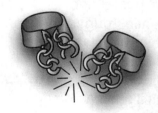

End to Slavery

Student Instructions: Amendments 16, 17, 18, and 19

Materials Needed

Glue, scissors, colored pencils

How to Create a Right-hand Interactive Notebook Page

Read the Key Details page. Then cut out the page and attach it to the right-hand page of your interactive notebook. Use what you have learned to create the left-hand page.

How to Create a Left-hand Interactive Notebook Page

Complete the following steps to create the left-hand page of your interactive notebook. Use lots of color.

Step 1: Cut out the title and glue it to the top of the notebook page.

Step 2: Cut out the four flap pieces. Apply glue to the back of the gray tabs and attach each flap piece below the title.

Step 3: Under each flap, write a brief summary of the amendment.

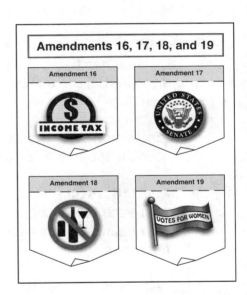

Demonstrate and Reflect on What You Have Learned

Some states had already given women the right to vote before the passage of the Nineteenth Amendment. Research the women's suffrage movement to find out the names of these states. List the states in your interactive notebook.

Key Details

Amendments 16, 17, 18, and 19

Many Americans in the early 1900s saw problems that needed fixing: the rich not paying their share of the cost of government, forests and wildlife being destroyed, corruption in government, children working in factories instead of going to school, alcohol damaging families, and the need for better schools and recreation. Reformers, called Progressives, began to work to improve America. Amendments 16, 17, 18, and 19 were a direct result of their efforts.

AMENDMENT 16: Income Tax [1913]
- Congress has the power to set and collect taxes on incomes without any regard for census.

  [*The federal government had relied mostly on tariffs and land sales to pay its expenses. The first regular income tax was levied in 1913 and now is the major source of government revenues. (Income tax had been levied during the Civil War era.)*]

AMENDMENT 17: Senators [1913]
- Each state has two senators elected by the people for six-year terms. Each senator has one vote. A person eligible to vote for the largest branch of the state legislature can vote for senators.
- When vacancies occur, the governor of the state issues an election notice to fill the vacancy; however, the state legislature can give the governor the authority to make temporary appointments until the next election when the people choose a new senator.

AMENDMENT 18: Prohibition [1919]
- Prohibits the manufacturing, selling, or transporting of intoxicating liquors within the United States and its territories.

  [*Amendment 18 was repealed by Amendment 21 in 1933.*]

AMENDMENT 19: Women's Suffrage [1920]
- Women cannot be denied the right to vote.

  [*Some states had already given women the right to vote, but this amendment gave all women the vote. It was the result of a long struggle on the part of the women's suffrage movement that had started in 1848.*]

Amendments 16, 17, 18, and 19

Amendment 16

Amendment 17

Amendment 18

Amendment 19

Student Instructions: Amendments 20 and 21

Materials Needed

Glue, scissors, colored pencils

How to Create a Right-hand Interactive Notebook Page

Read the Key Details page. Then cut out the page and attach it to the right-hand page of your interactive notebook. Use what you have learned to create the left-hand page.

How to Create a Left-hand Interactive Notebook Page

Complete the following steps to create the left-hand page of your interactive notebook. Use lots of color.

Step 1: Cut out the title and glue it to the top of the notebook page.

Step 2: Fill in the blanks on the Amendment 20 flap piece. Cut out the piece and apply glue to the back section above the fold line. Attach it below the title.

Step 3: Under the flap, summarize Section 3 of Amendment 20.

Step 4: Fill in the blanks on the Amendment 21 piece. Cut out the piece and apply glue to the back. Attach it at the bottom of the page.

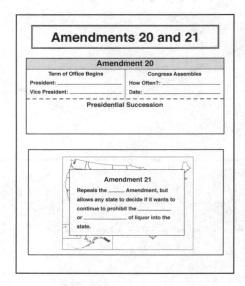

Demonstrate and Reflect on What You Have Learned

Go online at < https://www.youtube.com/watch?v=G1T8NlbZ71s> and watch the video *Bet You Didn't Know: Prohibition.* After watching the video, summarize the "noble experiment" in your interactive notebook.

Key Details

Amendments 20 and 21

Amendments 20 and 21 were added in 1933. Amendment 20 moved the date of the inauguration from March to January. Amendment 21 repealed the 18th Amendment.

AMENDMENT 20: Terms of Office and Succession [1933]
SECTION 1: Terms of President and Vice President

- The terms of president and vice president ends at noon on January 20, and the terms of senators and representatives at noon on January 3. Their successors' terms begin when theirs end.

SECTION 2: Congress Assembles
- Congress is to assemble at least once a year; that meeting begins on January 3 unless Congress chooses a different date.

SECTION 3: Presidential Succession
- If the president-elect dies before January 20, the vice president-elect becomes president.
- If a president has not been chosen by January 20 or if the president-elect fails to be qualified, the vice president-elect acts as president until the president is qualified.
- When neither the president-elect nor vice president-elect qualifies, the Congress decides who will act as president. That person acts until the president-elect or vice president-elect has qualified.

SECTION 4: Presidential Vacancy
- When the person the House of Representatives has selected as president is unable to fulfill the office and the person the Senate has designated as vice president is unable to assume the duties of the president, Congress passes legislation to handle the situation.

AMENDMENT 21: Prohibition Repealed [1933]
SECTION 1: Amendment 18 is now repealed.

SECTION 2: The transporting or importing of liquor into any state that chooses to continue prohibiting liquor is still prohibited.

Amendments 20 and 21

Amendment 20

Term of Office Begins

President: _____

Vice President: _____

Congress Assembles

How Often?: _____

Date: _____

Presidential Succession

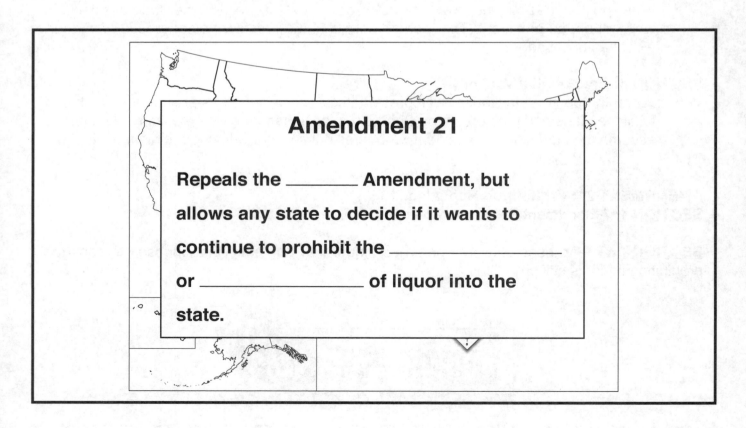

Amendment 21

Repeals the _____ Amendment, but

allows any state to decide if it wants to

continue to prohibit the _____

or _____ of liquor into the

state.

Student Instructions: Amendments 22, 23, and 24

Materials Needed

Glue, scissors, colored pencils

How to Create a Right-hand Interactive Notebook Page

Read the Key Details page. Then cut out the page and attach it to the right-hand page of your interactive notebook. Use what you have learned to create the left-hand page.

How to Create a Left-hand Interactive Notebook Page

Complete the following steps to create the left-hand page of your interactive notebook. Use lots of color.

Step 1: Cut out the title and glue it to the top of the notebook page.

Step 2: Cut out the triangle flap book. (If possible, enlarge the triangle pattern on a copier so the folded triangle has plenty of room for notes.)

Step 3: Cut apart the three amendment label pieces. Apply glue to the back of each of the three labels. Attach a label to each triangle flap next to the fold line with the words facing the flap's point.

Step 4: Turn the flap book over.

Step 5: Fold down the three amendment flaps to form one triangle-shaped flap book.

Sept 6: Apply glue to the gray triangle and attach the triangle-shaped flap book below the title. On the back of each flap, summarize the amendment.

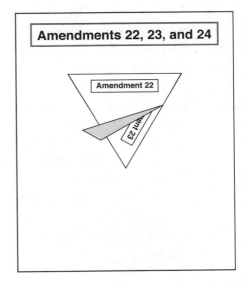

Demonstrate and Reflect on What You Have Learned

President Franklin D. Roosevelt was elected to four presidential terms, making him the longest-serving president. Go online or use reference sources to research Roosevelt's life. Write ten interesting facts about his life in your interactive notebook.

Key Details

Amendments 22, 23, and 24

Amendment 22 limits the president to two terms. Amendment 23 provides a way for citizens living in Washington, D.C. to have a voice in the selection of a president. Amendment 24 abolishes the poll tax.

AMENDMENT 22: Term of President [1951]
- No person can be elected president more than twice, and no one who has acted as president more than two years can be elected more than once.

  [*President Franklin Roosevelt had been elected four times. Many Americans felt that limits should be placed on the number of terms a president could serve. In the future, no president was to serve more than ten years.*]

AMENDMENT 23: Washington, D.C. [1961]
- The District of Columbia is to appoint by a method Congress directs: electors for president and vice president equal to the number of electors of the least populated state.
- Electors meet in the District and perform their duties.

  [*The Constitution did not provide a way for those who lived in the District of Columbia to vote for president. This amendment corrected that situation. Notice that it did not give them representation in Congress. They are now allowed a non-voting delegate to the U.S. House.*]

AMENDMENT 24: Poll Tax [1964]
- The right to vote for president and vice president, or for U.S. senator and representative in Congress, cannot be denied because the person has failed to pay a poll tax or other tax.

  [*Some southern states required a person to pay a poll tax before that person could vote. Collected several months before the election, it was a method of keeping the poor, especially African Americans, from voting.*]

Amendments 22, 23, and 24

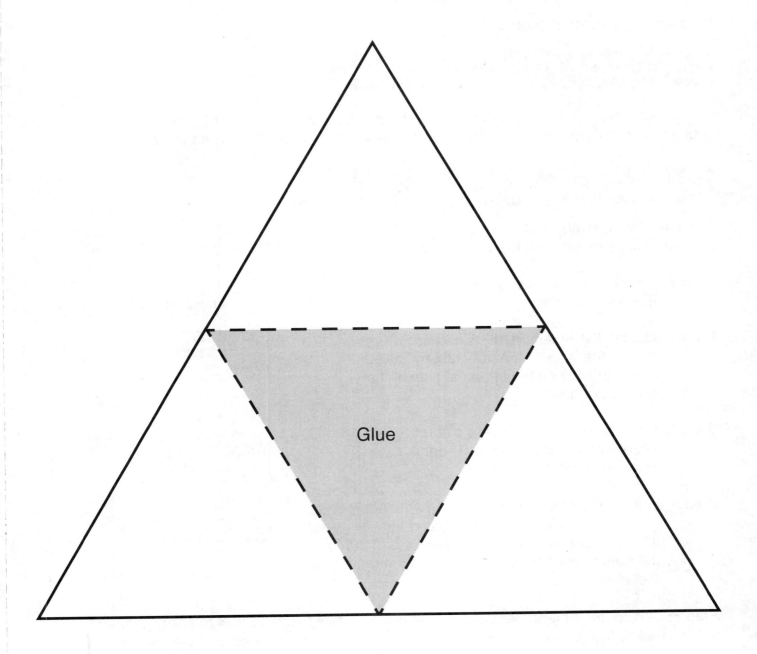

Glue

| Amendment 22 | Amendment 23 | Amendment 24 |

Student Instructions: Amendments 25, 26, and 27

Materials Needed

Glue, scissors, colored pencils

How to Create a Right-hand Interactive Notebook Page

Read the Key Details page. Then cut out the page and attach it to the right-hand page of your interactive notebook. Use what you have learned to create the left-hand page.

How to Create a Left-hand Interactive Notebook Page

Complete the following steps to create the left-hand page of your interactive notebook. Use lots of color.

Step 1: Cut out the title and glue it to the top of the notebook page.

Step 2: Cut out the Amendment 25 flap book. Apply glue to the back of the gray tab and attach it below the title on the left-hand side of the notebook page.

Step 3: On each box, summarize a different section of the amendment. Then accordion-fold the flap book.

Step 4: Cut out the Amendment 26 flap piece. Apply glue to the back of the gray tab and attach it below the title on the right-hand side of the the notebook page. Under the flap, summarize the amendment.

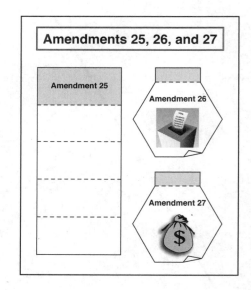

Step 5: Cut out the Amendment 27 flap piece. Apply glue to the back of the gray tab and attach it below the Amendment 26 flap piece. Under the flap, summarize the amendment.

Demonstrate and Reflect on What You Have Learned

The Presidential Succession Act of 1947 provides guidelines for the order of presidential succession. Research the order of presidential succession. Write the order in your interactive notebook.

Key Details

Amendments 25, 26, and 27

Amendment 25 establishes a procedure to follow in case a president dies, resigns, or is removed from office. It also determines who will be vice president when the office is vacant. Amendment 26 gave eighteen-year-olds the right to vote. Amendment 27 limits the ability of Congress to increase their pay.

AMENDMENT 25: Presidential Disability and Succession [1967]
SECTION 1: Replacing the President
- If the president is removed, dies, or resigns, the vice president becomes president.

SECTION 2: Replacing the Vice President
- Whenever there is no vice president, the president nominates a vice president who takes office after he has been confirmed by the U.S. Senate and House.

SECTION 3: Replacing the President With His Consent
- When the president informs the president pro tempore of the Senate and Speaker of the House in writing that he is unable to carry out the duties of his office, the vice president assumes the president's duties until the president is able to resume his duties.

SECTION 4: Replacing the President Without His Consent
- If the vice president and a majority of the cabinet or some other group inform the president pro tempore of the Senate and Speaker of the House in a written statement that the president is unable to carry out the powers and duties of his office, the vice president temporarily becomes acting president.
- When the president informs the president pro tempore and the Speaker in writing that no inability exists, he again resumes his office unless the vice president and a majority of the cabinet, or other body designated by law, inform the president pro tempore and the Speaker in writing that the president is unable to assume his responsibilities.
- Congress decides the issue and must assemble within 48 hours for that purpose if it is not already in session. It takes a two-thirds vote of both houses to decide that the president is unable to carry out his responsibilities; if that standard is met, the vice president continues to serve as acting president. Without a two-thirds majority in both houses, the president resumes the responsibilities of his office.

AMENDMENT 26: Eighteen-Year-Old Vote [1971]
- The right of citizens over the age of 18 years to vote cannot be denied on account of age.

AMENDMENT 27: Congressional Pay Raises [1992]
- Salaries for members of Congress cannot be changed until after the next election of representatives has occurred.

[Although this was one of the original amendments proposed in the Bill of Rights, it was not ratified until 1992.]

Amendments 25, 26, and 27

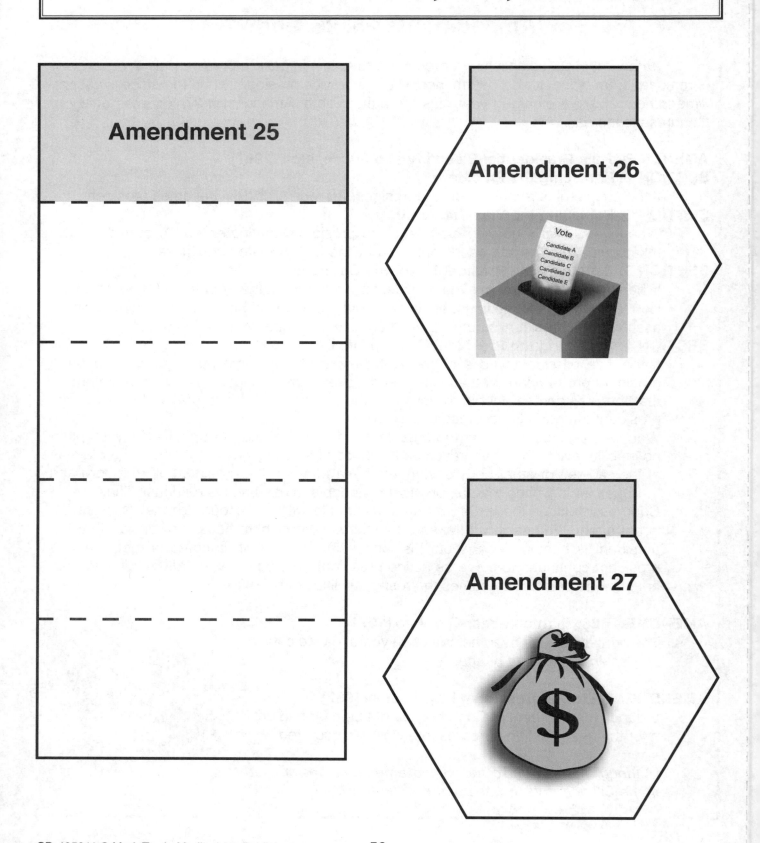

Amendment 25

Amendment 26

Amendment 27

The Constitution of the United States

(Italicized words indicate portions of the Constitution that are no longer in effect.)

Preamble

We the people of the United States, in Order to form a more perfect Union, establish Justice, insure domestic Tranquility, provide for the common defense, promote the general Welfare, and secure the Blessings of Liberty to ourselves and our Posterity, do ordain and establish this Constitution for the United States of America.

ARTICLE I   *(Legislature)*

Section 1. All legislative Powers herein granted shall be vested in a Congress of the United States, which shall consist of a Senate and House of Representatives.

(House of Representatives)

Section 2. The House of Representatives shall be composed of Members chosen every second Year by the People of the several States, and the Electors in each State shall have the Qualifications requisite for Electors of the most numerous Branch of the State Legislature.

(Qualifications for Representatives)

No Person shall be a Representative who shall not have attained to the Age of twenty five Years, and been seven Years a Citizen of the United States, and who shall not, when elected, be an Inhabitant of that State in which he shall be chosen.

(Method of Apportionment)

Representatives and direct Taxes shall be apportioned among the several States which may be included within this Union, according to their respective Numbers, *which shall be determined by adding to the whole Number of free Persons, including those bound to Service for a Term of Years, and excluding Indians not taxed, three fifths of all other Persons.* The actual Enumeration shall be made within three Years after the first Meeting of the Congress of the United States, and within every subsequent Term of ten Years, in such Manner as they shall by Law direct. The Number of Representatives shall not exceed one for every thirty Thousand, but each state shall have at Least one Representative; *and until such enumeration shall be made, the State of New Hampshire shall be entitled to choose three, Massachusetts eight, Rhode Island and Providence Plantations one, Connecticut five, New York six, New Jersey four, Pennsylvania eight, Delaware one, Maryland six, Virginia ten, North Carolina five, South Carolina five, and Georgia three.*

(Vacancies)

When vacancies happen in the Representation from any State, the Executive Authority thereof shall issue Writs of Election to fill such Vacancies.

(Rules of the House, Impeachment)

The House of Representatives shall choose their Speaker and other Officers; and shall have the sole Power of Impeachment.

(Senators)

Section 3. The Senate of the United States shall be composed of two Senators from each State, *chosen by the Legislature thereof,* for six Years; and each Senator shall have one Vote.

Immediately after they shall be assembled in Consequence of the first Election, they shall be divided as equally as may be into three Classes. The Seats of the Senators of the first Class shall be vacated at the Expiration of the second Year, of the second Class at the Expiration of the fourth Year, and of the third Class at the Expiration of the sixth Year, so that one third may be chosen every second Year; *and if Vacancies happen by Resignation, or otherwise, during the Recess of the Legislature of any State, the Executive thereof may make temporary Appointments until the next Meeting of the Legislature, which shall then fill such Vacancies.*

(Qualifications of Senators)

No Person shall be a Senator who shall not have attained to the Age of thirty Years, and been nine Years a Citizen of the United States, and who shall not, when elected, be an Inhabitant of that State for which he shall be chosen.

(Vice President)

The Vice President of the United States shall be President of the Senate, but shall have no Vote, unless they be equally divided.

The Senate shall choose their other Officers, and also a President *pro tempore,* in the Absence of the Vice President, or when he shall exercise the Office of President of the United States.

(Impeachments)

The Senate shall have the sole Power to try all Impeachments. When sitting for that Purpose, they shall be on Oath or Affirmation. When the President of the United States is tried, the Chief Justice shall preside: And no Person shall be convicted without the Concurrence of two thirds of the Members present.

Judgment in Cases of Impeachment shall not extend further than to removal from Office, and disqualification to hold and enjoy any Office of honor, Trust or Profit under the United States: but the Party convicted shall nevertheless be liable and subject to Indictment, Trial, Judgment and Punishment, according to Law.

(Elections)

Section 4. The Times, Places and Manner of holding Elections for Senators and Representatives, shall be prescribed in each State by the Legislature thereof; but the Congress may at any time by Law make or alter such Regulations, except as to the places of choosing Senators.

(Sessions)

The Congress shall assemble at least once in every Year, and such Meeting *shall be on the first Monday in December, unless they shall by Law appoint a different Day.*

(Proceedings of the House and the Senate)

Section 5. Each House shall be the Judge of the Elections, Returns and Qualifications of its own Members, and a Majority of each shall constitute a Quorum to do Business; but a smaller Number may adjourn from day to day, and may be authorized to compel the Attendance of absent Members, in such Manner, and under such Penalties, as each House may provide.

Each House may determine the Rules of its Proceedings, punish its Members for disorderly Behavior, and, with the Concurrence of two thirds, expel a Member.

Each House shall keep a Journal of its Proceedings, and from time to time publish the same, excepting such Parts as may in their Judgment require Secrecy; and the Yeas and Nays of the Members of either House on any question shall, at the Desire of one fifth of those Present, be entered on the Journal.

Neither House, during the Session of Congress, shall, without the Consent of the other, adjourn for more than three days, nor to any other Place than that in which the two Houses shall be sitting.

(Members' Compensation and Privileges)

Section 6. The Senators and Representatives shall receive a Compensation for their Services, to be ascertained by Law, and paid out of the Treasury of the United States. They shall in all Cases, except Treason, Felony and Breach of the Peace, be privileged from Arrest during their Attendance at the Session of their respective Houses, and in going to and returning from the same; and for any Speech or Debate in either House, they shall not be questioned in any other Place.

No Senator or Representative shall, during the Time for which he was elected, be appointed to any civil Office under the Authority of the United States, which shall have been created, or the Emoluments whereof shall have been increased during such time; and no Person holding any Office under the United States, shall be a Member of either House during his Continuance in Office.

(Money Bills)

Section 7. All Bills for raising Revenue shall originate in the House of Representatives; but the Senate may propose or concur with Amendments as on other Bills.

(Presidential Veto and Congressional Power to Override)

Every Bill which shall have passed the House of Representatives and the Senate, shall, before it becomes a Law, be presented to the President of the United States; If he approves he shall sign it, but if not he shall return it, with his Objections to that House in which it shall have originated, who shall enter the Objections at large on their Journal, and proceed to reconsider it. If after such Reconsideration two thirds of that House shall agree to pass the Bill, it shall be sent, together with the Objections, to the other House, by which it shall likewise be reconsidered, and if approved by two thirds of that House, it shall become a Law. But in all such Cases the Votes of both Houses shall be determined by yeas and Nays, and the Names of the Persons voting for and against the Bill shall be entered on the Journal of each House respectively. If any Bill shall not be returned by the President within ten Days (Sundays excepted) after it shall have been presented to him, the Same shall be a Law, in like Manner as if he had signed it, unless the Congress by their Adjournment prevent its Return, in which Case it shall not be a Law.

Every Order, Resolution, or Vote to which the Concurrence of the Senate and House of Representatives may be necessary (except on a question of Adjournment) shall be presented to the President of the United States; and before the Same shall take Effect, shall be approved by him, or being disapproved by him, shall be repassed by two thirds of the Senate and House of Representatives, according to the Rules and Limitations prescribed in the Case of a Bill.

(Congressional Powers)
Section 8. The Congress shall have Power

To lay and collect Taxes, Duties, Imposts and Excises, to pay the Debts and provide for the common Defense and general Welfare of the United States; but all Duties, Imposts and Excises shall be uniform throughout the United States;

To borrow Money on the credit of the United States;

To regulate Commerce with foreign Nations, and among the several States, and with the Indian tribes;

To establish an uniform Rule of Naturalization, and uniform Laws on the subject of Bankruptcies throughout the United States;

To coin Money, regulate the Value thereof, and of foreign Coin, and fix the Standard of Weights and Measures;

To provide for the Punishment of counterfeiting the Securities and current Coin of the United States;

To establish Post Offices and post Roads;

To promote the Progress of Science and useful Arts, by securing for limited Times to Authors and Inventors the exclusive Right to their respective Writings and Discoveries;

To constitute Tribunals inferior to the supreme Court;

To define and punish Piracies and Felonies committed on the high Seas, and Offenses against the Law of Nations;

To declare War, grant Letters of Marque and Reprisal, and make Rules concerning Captures on Land and Water;

To raise and support Armies, but no Appropriation of Money to that Use shall be for a longer Term than two Years;

To provide and maintain a Navy;

To make Rules for the Government and Regulation of the land and naval Forces;

To provide for calling forth the Militia to execute the Laws of the Union, suppress Insurrections and repel Invasions;

To provide for organizing, arming, and disciplining, the Militia, and for governing such Part of them as may be employed in the Service of the United States, reserving to the States respectively the Appointment of the Officers, and the Authority of training the Militia according to the discipline prescribed by Congress;

To exercise exclusive Legislation in all Cases whatsoever, over such District (not exceeding ten Miles square) as may, by Cession of particular States, and the Acceptance of Congress, become the Seat of Government of the United States, and to exercise like Authority over all Places purchased by the Consent of the Legislature of the State in which the same shall be, for the Erection of Forts, Magazines, Arsenals, Dockyards, and other needful Buildings;—And

To make all Laws which shall be necessary and proper for carrying into Execution the foregoing Powers, and all other Powers vested by this Constitution in the Government of the United States, or in any Department or Officer thereof.

(Limits on Congressional Power)
Section 9. *The Migration or Importation of such Persons as any of the States now existing shall think proper to admit, shall not be prohibited by the Congress prior to the Year one thousand eight hundred and eight; but a Tax or duty may be imposed on such Importation, not exceeding ten dollars for each Person.*

The Privilege of the Writ of Habeas Corpus shall not be suspended, unless when in cases of Rebellion or Invasion the public Safety may require it.

No Bill of Attainder or ex post facto Law shall be passed.

No Capitation, or other direct, Tax shall be laid, unless in Proportion to the Census or Enumeration herein before directed to be taken.

No Tax or Duty shall be laid on Articles exported from any State.

No Preference shall be given by any Regulation of Commerce or Revenue to the Ports of one State over those of another: nor shall Vessels bound to, or from, one State, be obliged to enter, clear, or pay Duties in another.

No Money shall be drawn from the Treasury, but in Consequence of Appropriations made by law; and a regular Statement and Account of the Receipts and

Expenditures of all public Money shall be published from time to time.

No Title of Nobility shall be granted by the United States: And no Person holding any Office of Profit or Trust under them, shall, without the Consent of the Congress, accept of any present, Emolument, Office, or Title, of any kind whatever, from any King, Prince, or foreign State.

(Limits on Powers of the States)

Section 10. No State shall enter into any Treaty, Alliance, or Confederation; grant letters of Marque and Reprisal; coin Money, emit Bills of Credit; make any Thing but gold and silver Coin a Tender in Payment of Debts; pass any Bill of Attainder, ex post facto Law, or Law impairing the Obligation of Contracts, or grant any Title of Nobility.

No State shall, without the Consent of Congress, lay any Imposts or Duties on Imports or Exports, except what may be absolutely necessary for executing its inspection Laws: and the net Produce of all Duties and Imposts, laid by any State on Imports or Exports, shall be for the Use of the Treasury of the United States; and all such Laws shall be subject to the Revision and Control of the Congress.

No State shall, without the Consent of Congress, lay any Duty of Tonnage, keep Troops, or Ships of War in time of Peace, enter into any Agreement or Compact with another State, or with a foreign Power, or engage in War, unless actually invaded, or in such imminent Danger as will not admit of delay.

ARTICLE II   (Executive)

(President)

Section 1. The executive Power shall be vested in a President of the United States of America. He shall hold his Office during the Term of four Years, and, together with the Vice President, chosen for the same Term, be elected as follows

(Election of President)

Each State shall appoint, in such Manner as the Legislature thereof may direct, a Number of Electors, equal to the whole Number of Senators and Representatives to which the State may be entitled in the Congress: but no Senator or Representative, or Person holding an Office of Trust or Profit under the United States, shall be appointed an Elector.

(Electors)

The Electors shall meet in their respective States, and vote by Ballot for two Persons, of whom one at least shall not be an inhabitant of the same State with themselves. And they shall make a List of all the Persons voted for, and of the Number of Votes for each; which List they shall sign and certify, and transmit sealed to the Seat of Government of the United States, directed to the President of the Senate. The President of the Senate shall, in the Presence of the Senate and House of Representatives, open all the Certificates, and the votes shall then be counted. The Person having the greatest Number of Votes shall be the President, if such Number be a Majority of the whole Number of Electors appointed; and if there be more than one who have such Majority, and have an equal Number of votes, then the House of Representatives shall immediately choose by Ballot one of them for President; and if no Person have a Majority, then from the five highest on the List the said House shall in like Manner choose the President. But in choosing the President, the Votes shall be taken by States, the Representation from each State having one Vote; A quorum for this purpose shall consist of a Member or Members from two thirds of the States, and a Majority of all the States shall be necessary to a Choice. In every Case, after the Choice of the President, the Person having the greatest Number of Votes of the Electors shall be the Vice President. But if there should remain two or more who have equal votes, the Senate shall choose from them by Ballot the Vice President.

The Congress may determine the Time of choosing the Electors, and the day on which they shall give their Votes; which Day shall be the same throughout the United States.

(Qualifications of President)

No person except a natural born Citizen, *or a Citizen of the United States, at the time of the Adoption of this Constitution,* shall be eligible to the Office of President; neither shall any Person be eligible to that Office who shall not have attained to the Age of thirty five Years, and been fourteen Years a Resident within the United States.

(Succession to the Presidency)

In Case of the removal of the President from Office, or of his Death, Resignation, or Inability to discharge the Powers and Duties of the said Office, the Same shall devolve on the Vice President, and the Congress may by Law provide for the Case of Removal, Death, Resignation, or Inability, both of the President and Vice President, declaring what Officer shall then act as President, and such Officer shall act accordingly, until the Disability be removed, or a President shall be elected.

(Compensation)

The President shall, at stated Times, receive for his Services, a Compensation, which shall neither be increased nor diminished during the Period for which he shall have been elected, and he shall not receive within that Period any other Emolument from the United States, or any of them.

(Oath of Office)

Before he enter on the Execution of his office, he shall take the following Oath or Affirmation:—"I do solemnly swear (or affirm) that I will faithfully execute the Office of the President of the United States, and will to the best of my Ability, preserve, protect and defend the Constitution of the United States."

(Powers of the President)

Section 2. The President shall be Commander in Chief of the Army and Navy of the United States, and of the Militia of the several States, when called into the actual Service of the United States; he may require the Opinion, in writing, of the principal Officer in each of the executive Departments, upon any Subject relating to the Duties of their respective Offices, and he shall have Power to grant Reprieves and Pardons for Offenses against the United States, except in Cases of Impeachment.

(Making of Treaties)

He shall have Power, by and with the Advice and Consent of the Senate, to make Treaties, provided two thirds of the Senators present concur; and he shall nominate, and by and with the Advice and Consent of the Senate, shall appoint Ambassadors, other public Ministers and Consuls, Judges of the supreme Court, and all other Officers of the United States, whose Appointments are not herein otherwise provided for, and which shall be established by Law: but Congress may by Law vest the Appointment of such inferior Officers, as they think proper, in the President alone, in the Courts of Law, or in the Heads of Departments.

(Vacancies)

The President shall have Power to fill up all Vacancies that may happen during the Recess of the Senate, by granting Commissions which shall expire at the End of their next Session.

(Additional Duties and Powers)

Section 3. He shall from time to time give to the Congress Information of the State of the Union, and recommend to their Consideration such Measures as he shall judge necessary and expedient; he may, on extraordinary Occasions, convene both Houses, or either of them, and in Case of Disagreement between them, with Respect to the Time of Adjournment, he may adjourn them to such Time as he shall think proper; he shall receive Ambassadors and other public Ministers; he shall take Care that the Laws be faithfully executed, and shall Commission all the Officers of the United States.

(Impeachment)

Section 4. The President, Vice President and all civil Officers of the United States shall be removed from Office on Impeachment for, and Conviction of, Treason, Bribery, or other high Crimes and Misdemeanors.

ARTICLE III *(Judiciary)*

(Courts, Judges, Compensation)

Section 1. The judicial Power of the United States, shall be vested in one supreme Court, and in such inferior Courts as the Congress may from time to time ordain and establish. The Judges, both of the supreme and inferior Courts, shall hold their Offices during good Behavior, and shall, at stated Times, receive for their Services, a Compensation which shall not be diminished during their Continuance in Office.

(Jurisdiction)

Section 2. The judicial Power shall extend to all Cases, in Law and Equity, arising under this Constitution, the Laws of the United States, and Treaties made, or which shall be made, under their Authority—to all Cases affecting Ambassadors, other public Ministers and Consuls;—to all Cases of admiralty and maritime Jurisdiction;—to Controversies to which the United States shall be a Party;—to Controversies between two or more States;—*between a State and Citizens of another State;*—between

Citizens of different States;—between Citizens of the same State claiming Lands under Grants of different States, and between a State, or the Citizens thereof, and foreign States, Citizens or Subjects.

In all Cases affecting Ambassadors, other public Ministers and Consuls, and those in which a State shall be Party, the Supreme Court shall have original Jurisdiction. In all the other Cases before mentioned, the supreme Court shall have appellate Jurisdiction, both as to Law and Fact, with such Exceptions, and under such Regulations as the Congress shall make.

(Trial by Jury)

The Trial of all Crimes, except in Cases of Impeachment, shall be by Jury; and such Trial shall be held in the State where said Crimes shall have been committed; but when not committed within any State, the Trial shall be at such Place or Places as the Congress may by Law have directed.

(Treason)

Section 3. Treason against the United States, shall consist only in levying War against them, or in adhering to their Enemies, giving them Aid and Comfort. No Person shall be convicted of Treason unless on the Testimony of two Witnesses to the same overt Act, or on Confession in open Court.

The Congress shall have Power to declare the Punishment of Treason, but no Attainder of Treason shall work Corruption of Blood, or Forfeiture except during the Life of the Person attained.

ARTICLE IV   (Federal System)

Section 1. Full Faith and Credit shall be given in each State to the public Acts, Records, and judicial Proceedings of every other State. And the Congress may by general Laws prescribe the Manner in which such Acts, Records, and Proceedings shall be proved, and the Effect thereof.

(Privileges and Immunities of Citizens)

Section 2. The Citizens of each State shall be entitled to all Privileges and Immunities of Citizens in the several States.

A Person charged in any State with Treason, Felony, or other Crime, who shall flee from Justice, and be found in another State, shall on Demand of the executive Authority of the State from which he fled, be delivered up, to be removed to the State having Jurisdiction of the crime.

No Person held to Service or Labor in one State, under the Laws thereof, escaping into another, shall, in Consequence of any Law or Regulation therein, be discharged from such Service or Labor, but shall be delivered up on Claim of the Party to whom such Service or Labor may be due.

(Admission and Formation of New States; Governing of Territories)

Section 3. New States may be admitted by the Congress into this Union; but no new State shall be formed or erected within the Jurisdiction of any other State; nor any State be formed by the Junction of two or more States, or Parts of States, without the Consent of the Legislatures of the States concerned as well as of the Congress.

The Congress shall have Power to dispose of and make all needful Rules and Regulations respecting the Territory or other Property belonging to the United States; and nothing in this Constitution shall be so construed as to Prejudice any Claims of the United States, or of any particular State.

(Federal Protection of the States)

Section 4. The United States shall guarantee to every State in this Union a Republican Form of Government, and shall protect each of them against Invasion; and on Application of the Legislature, or of the Executive (when the Legislature cannot be convened), against domestic Violence.

ARTICLE V   (Amendments)

The Congress, whenever two thirds of both Houses shall deem it necessary, shall propose Amendments to this Constitution, or, on the Application of the Legislatures of two thirds of the several States, shall call a Convention for proposing Amendments, which, in either Case, shall be valid to all Intents and Purposes, as Part of this Constitution, when ratified by the legislatures of three fourths of the several States, or by Conventions in three fourths thereof, as the one or the other Mode of Ratification may be proposed by the Congress; Provided *that no Amendments which may be made prior to the Year One thousand eight hundred and eight shall in any Manner affect the first and fourth Clauses in the Ninth Section of the first Article; and* that no State, without its Consent, shall be deprived of its equal Suffrage in the Senate.

ARTICLE VI   *(Constitution as Supreme Law)*

All Debts contracted and Engagements entered into, before the Adoption of this Constitution, shall be as valid against the United States under this Constitution, as under the Confederation.

This Constitution, and the Laws of the United States which shall be made in Pursuance thereof; and all Treaties made, or which shall be made, under the Authority of the United States, shall be the supreme Law of the Land, and the Judges in every State shall be bound thereby, any Thing in the Constitution or Laws of any State to the Contrary notwithstanding.

The Senators and Representatives before mentioned, and the Members of the several State Legislatures, and all executive and judicial Officers, both of the United States and of the several States, shall be bound by Oath or Affirmation, to support this Constitution; but no religious Test shall ever be required as a Qualification to any Office or public Trust under the United States.

ARTICLE VII   *(Ratification)*

The Ratification of the Conventions of nine States shall be sufficient for the Establishment of the Constitution between the States so ratifying the same.

Done in Convention by the Unanimous Consent of the States present, the Seventeenth Day of September in the Year of our Lord one thousand seven hundred and Eighty seven and of the Independence of the United States of America the Twelfth. In witness whereof We have hereunto subscribed our Names.

Geo. Washington, *President and deputy from Virginia; Attest* William Jackson, *Secretary; Delaware:* Geo. Read, Gunning Bedford, Jr., John Dickinson, Richard Bassett, Jaco. Broom; *Maryland:* James McHenry, Daniel of St. Thomas Jenifer, Danl. Carroll; *Virginia:* John Blair, James Madison, Jr.; *North Carolina:* Wm. Blount, Richd. Dobbs Spaight, Hu Williamson; *South Carolina:* J. Rutledge, Charles Cotesworth Pinckney, Charles Pinckney, Pierce Butler; *Georgia:* William Few, Abr. Baldwin; *New Hampshire:* John Langdon, Nicholas Gilman; *Massachusetts:* Nathaniel Gorham, Rufus King; *Connecticut:* Wm. Saml. Johnson, Roger Sherman; *New York:* Alexander Hamilton; *New Jersey:* Wil. Livingston, David Brearley, Wm. Paterson, Jona. Dayton; *Pennsylvania:* B. Franklin, Thomas Mifflin, Robt. Morris, Geo. Clymer, Thos. FitzSimons, Jared Ingersoll, James Wilson, Gouv. Morris.

AMENDMENTS TO THE CONSTITUTION
(The first ten amendments are known as the Bill of Rights.)

AMENDMENT I [1791]   *(Freedoms)*

(Speech, Press, Assembly, and Petition)

Congress shall make no law respecting an establishment of religion, or prohibiting the free exercise thereof; or abridging the freedom of speech, or of the press; or the right of the people peaceably to assemble, and to petition the Government for a redress of grievances.

AMENDMENT II [1791]   *(Right to Bear Arms)*

A well regulated Militia, being necessary to the security of a free State, the right of the people to keep and bear Arms, shall not be infringed.

AMENDMENT III [1791]   *(Quartering of Soldiers)*

No Soldier shall, in time of peace be quartered in any house, without the consent of the Owner, nor in time of war, but in a manner to be prescribed by law.

AMENDMENT IV [1791]   *(Freedom of Persons)*

(Warrants, Searches, and Seizure)

The right of the people to be secure in their persons, houses, papers, and effects, against unreasonable searches and seizures, shall not be violated, and no Warrants shall issue, but upon probable cause, supported by Oath or Affirmation, and particularly describing the place to be searched, and the persons or things to be seized.

AMENDMENT V [1791]   *(Capital Crimes)*

(Protection of the Accused; Compensation)

No person shall be held to answer for a capital, or otherwise infamous crime, unless on a presentment or indictment of a Grand Jury, except in cases arising in the land or naval forces, or in the Militia, when in actual service in time of War or public danger; nor shall any person be subject for the same offense to be twice put in jeopardy of life or limb; nor shall be compelled in any criminal case to be a witness against himself, nor be deprived of life, liberty, or property, without due process of law; nor shall private property be taken for public use, without just compensation.

AMENDMENT VI [1791]　　　(Trial by Jury)

(Accusation, Witnesses, Counsel)

In all criminal prosecutions, the accused shall enjoy the right to a speedy and public trial, by an impartial jury of the State and district wherein the crime shall have been committed, which district shall have been previously ascertained by law, and to be informed of the nature and cause of the accusation; to be confronted with the witnesses against him; to have compulsory process for obtaining Witnesses in his favor, and to have the assistance of counsel for his defense.

AMENDMENT VII [1791]　　　(Civil Law)

In Suits at common law, where the value in controversy shall exceed twenty dollars, the right of trial by jury shall be preserved, and no fact tried by a jury, shall be otherwise re-examined in any court of the United States, than according to the rules of the common law.

AMENDMENT VIII [1791]　　　(Bails, Fines, and Punishments)

Excessive bail shall not be required, nor excessive fines imposed, nor cruel and unusual punishments inflicted.

AMENDMENT IX [1791]　　　(Rights Retained by the People)

The enumeration in the Constitution, of certain rights, shall not be construed to deny or disparage others retained by the people.

AMENDMENT X [1791]　　　(Rights Reserved to the States)

The powers not delegated to the United States by the Constitution, nor prohibited by it to the States, are reserved to the States respectively, or to the people.

AMENDMENT XI [1798]　　　(Jurisdictional Limits)

The Judicial power of the United States shall not be construed to extend to any suit in law or equity, commenced or prosecuted against one of the United States by Citizens of another State, or by Citizens or Subjects of any Foreign State.

AMENDMENT XII [1804]　　　(Electoral College)

The Electors shall meet in their respective States, and vote by ballot for President and Vice-President, one of whom, at least, shall not be an inhabitant of the same State with themselves; they shall name in their ballots the person voted for as President, and in distinct ballots the person voted for as Vice-President, and they shall make distinct lists of all persons voted for as President, and of all persons voted for as Vice-President, and of the number of votes for each, which lists they shall sign and certify, and transmit sealed to the seat of the government of the United States, directed to the President of the Senate;—The President of the Senate shall, in the presence of the Senate and House of Representatives, open all the certificates and the votes shall then be counted;—The person having the greatest number of votes for President, shall be the President, if such number be a majority of the whole number of Electors appointed; and if no person have such majority, then from the persons having the highest numbers not exceeding three on the list of those voted for as President, the House of Representatives shall choose immediately, by ballot, the President. But in choosing the President, the votes shall be taken by states, the representation from each state having one vote; a quorum for this purpose shall consist of a member or members from two-thirds of the states, and a majority of all the states shall be necessary to a choice. And if the House of Representatives shall not choose a President whenever the right of choice shall devolve upon them, before *the fourth day of March* next following, then the Vice-President shall act as President, as in the case of the death or other constitutional disability of the President.—The person having the greatest number of votes as Vice-President, shall be the Vice-President, if such number be a majority of the whole number of electors appointed, and if no person have a majority, then from the two highest numbers on the list, the Senate shall choose the Vice-President; a quorum for the purpose shall consist of two-thirds of the whole number of Senators, and a majority of the whole number shall be necessary to a choice. But no person constitutionally ineligible to the office of President shall be eligible to that of Vice-President of the United States.

AMENDMENT XIII [1865] *(Abolition of Slavery)*

Section 1. Neither slavery nor involuntary servitude, except as a punishment for crime whereof the party shall have been duly convicted, shall exist within the United States, or any place subject to their jurisdiction.

Section 2. Congress shall have power to enforce this article by appropriate legislation.

AMENDMENT XIV [1868] *(Citizenship)*

(Due Process of Law)

Section 1. All persons born or naturalized in the United States, and subject to the jurisdiction thereof, are citizens of the United States and of the State wherein they reside. No State shall make or enforce any law which shall abridge the privileges or immunities of citizens of the United States; nor shall any State deprive any person of life, liberty, or property, without due process of law; nor deny to any person within its jurisdiction the equal protection of the laws.

(Apportionment; Right to Vote)

Section 2. Representatives shall be apportioned among the several States according to their respective numbers, counting the whole number of persons in each State, excluding Indians not taxed. But when the right to vote at any election for the choice of electors for President and Vice President of the United States, Representatives in Congress, the Executive and Judicial officers of a State, or the members of the Legislature thereof, is denied to any of the male inhabitants of such State, being twenty-one years of age, and citizens of the United States, or in any way abridged, except for participation in rebellion, or other crime, the basis of representation therein shall be reduced in the proportion which the number of such male citizens shall bear to the whole number of male citizens twenty-one years of age in such State.

(Disqualification for Office)

Section 3. No person shall be a Senator or Representative in Congress, or elector of President and Vice President, or hold any office, civil or military, under the United States, or under any State, who, having previously taken an oath, as a member of Congress, or as an officer of the United States, or as a member of any State legislature, or as an executive or judicial officer of any State, to support the Constitution of the United States, shall have engaged in insurrection or rebellion against the same, or given aid or comfort to the enemies thereof. But Congress may by a vote of two-thirds of each House, remove such disability.

(Public Debt)

Section 4. The validity of the public debt of the United States, authorized by law, including debts incurred for payment of pensions and bounties for services in suppressing insurrection or rebellion, shall not be questioned. But neither the United States nor any State shall assume or pay any debt or obligation incurred in aid of insurrection or rebellion against the United States, or any claim for the loss of emancipation of any slave; but all such debts, obligations and claims shall be held illegal and void.

Section 5. The Congress shall have power to enforce, by appropriate legislation, the provisions of this article.

AMENDMENT XV [1870] *(Right to Vote)*

Section 1. The right of citizens of the United States to vote shall not be denied or abridged by the United States or by any State on account of race, color, or previous condition of servitude.

Section 2. The Congress shall have power to enforce this article by appropriate legislation.

AMENDMENT XVI [1913] *(Income Tax)*

The Congress shall have power to lay and collect taxes on incomes, from whatever source derived, without apportionment among the several States, and without regard to any census or enumeration.

AMENDMENT XVII [1913] (Senators)

(Election)

The Senate of the United States shall be composed of two Senators from each State, elected by the people thereof, for six years; and each Senator shall have one vote. The electors in each State shall have the qualifications requisite for electors of [voters for] the most numerous branch of the State legislatures.

(Vacancies)

When vacancies happen in the representation of any State in the Senate, the executive authority of such State shall issue writs of election to fill such vacancies: Provided, That the legislature of any State may empower the executive thereof to make temporary appointments until the people fill the vacancies by election as the legislature may direct.

This amendment shall not be so construed as to affect the election or term of any Senator chosen before it becomes valid as part of the Constitution.

AMENDMENT XVIII [1919] (Prohibition)

Section 1. After one year from the ratification of this article the manufacture, sale, or transportation of intoxicating liquors within, the importation thereof into, or the exportation thereof from the United States and all territory subject to the jurisdiction thereof for beverage purposes is hereby prohibited.

Section 2. The Congress and the several States shall have concurrent power to enforce this article by appropriate legislation.

Section 3. This article shall be inoperative unless it shall have been ratified as an amendment to the Constitution by the legislatures of the several States, as provided by the Constitution, within seven years from the date of the submission thereof to the States by the Congress.

AMENDMENT XIX [1920] (Women's Suffrage)

The right of citizens of the United States to vote shall not be denied or abridged by the United States or by any State on account of sex.

Congress shall have power to enforce this article by appropriate legislation.

AMENDMENT XX [1933] (Terms of Office)

Section 1. The terms of the President and Vice President shall end at noon on the 20th day of January, and the terms of Senators and Representatives at noon on the 3d day of January, of the years in which such terms would have ended if this article had not been ratified; and the terms of their successors shall then begin.

Section 2. The Congress shall assemble at least once in every year, and such meeting shall begin at noon on the 3d day of January, unless they shall by law appoint a different day.

(Succession)

Section 3. If, at the time fixed for the beginning of the term of the President, the President elect shall have died, the Vice President elect shall become President. If a President shall not have been chosen before the time fixed for the beginning of his term, or if the President elect shall have failed to qualify, then the Vice President elect shall act as President until a President shall have qualified; and the Congress may by law provide for the case wherein neither a President elect nor a Vice President elect shall have qualified, declaring who shall then act as President, or the manner in which one who is to act shall be selected, and such persons shall act accordingly until a President or Vice President shall have qualified.

Section 4. The Congress may by law provide for the case of the death of any of the persons from whom the House of Representatives may choose a President whenever the right of choice shall have devolved upon them, and for the case of the death of any of the persons from whom the Senate may choose a Vice President whenever the right of choice shall have devolved upon them.

Section 5. Sections 1 and 2 shall take effect on the 15th day of October following the ratification of this article.

Section 6. This article shall be inoperative unless it shall have been ratified as an amendment to the Constitution by the legislatures of three-fourths of the several States within seven years from the date of its submission.

AMENDMENT XXI [1933]   *(Prohibition Repealed)*

Section 1. The eighteenth article of amendment to the Constitution of the United States is hereby repealed.

Section 2. The transportation or importation into any State, Territory, or Possession of the United States for delivery or use therein of intoxicating liquors, in violation of the laws thereof, is hereby prohibited.

Section 3. This article shall be inoperative unless it shall have been ratified as an amendment to the Constitution by conventions in the several States, as provided in the Constitution, within seven years from the date of submission thereof to the States by the Congress.

AMENDMENT XXII [1951]   *(Term of President)*

Section 1. No person shall be elected to the office of the President more than twice, and no person who has held the office of President, or acted as President, for more than two years of a term to which some other person was elected President shall be elected to the office of the President more than once. But this Article shall not apply to any person holding the office of President when this Article was proposed by the Congress, and shall not prevent any person who may be holding the office of President, or acting as President, during the term within which this Article becomes operative from holding the office of President or acting as President during the remainder of such term.

Section 2. This article shall be inoperative unless it shall have been ratified as an amendment to the Constitution by the legislatures of three-fourths of the several States within seven years from the date of its submission to the States by the Congress.

AMENDMENT XXIII [1961]   *(Washington, D.C.)*

(Enfranchisement of Voters in Federal Elections)

Section 1. The District constituting the seat of Government of the United States shall appoint in such manner as the Congress may direct:

A number of electors of President and Vice President equal to the whole number of Senators and Representatives in Congress to which the District would be entitled if it were a State, but in no event more than the least populous State; they shall be in addition to those appointed by the States, but they shall be considered for the purposes of the election of President and Vice President, to be electors appointed by a State; and they shall meet in the District and perform such duties as provided by the twelfth article of amendment.

Section 2. The Congress shall have power to enforce this article by appropriate legislation.

AMENDMENT XXIV [1964]   *(Poll Tax)*

Section 1. The right of citizens of the United States to vote in any primary or other election for President or Vice President, for electors for President or Vice President, or for Senator or Representatives in Congress, shall not be denied or abridged by the United States or any State by reason of failure to pay any poll tax or other tax.

Section 2. The Congress shall have power to enforce this article by appropriate legislation.

AMENDMENT XXV [1967]   *(Succession)*

Section 1. In case of the removal of the President from office or of his death or resignation, the Vice President shall become President.

Section 2. Whenever there is a vacancy in the office of the Vice President, the President shall nominate a Vice President who shall take office upon confirmation by a majority vote of both Houses of Congress.

Section 3. Whenever the President transmits to the President pro tempore of the Senate and the Speaker of the House of Representatives his written declaration that he is unable to discharge the powers and duties of his office, and until he transmits to them a written declaration to the contrary, such powers and duties shall be discharged by the Vice President as Acting President.

Section 4. Whenever the Vice President and a majority of either the principal officers of the executive departments or of such other body as Congress may by law provide, transmit to the President pro tempore of the Senate and the Speaker of the House of Representatives their written declaration that the President is unable to discharge the powers and duties of his office, the Vice President shall immediately assume the powers and duties of the office as Acting President.

Thereafter, when the President transmits to the President pro tempore of the Senate and the

Speaker of the House of Representatives his written declaration that no inability exists, he shall resume the powers and duties of his office unless the Vice President and a majority of either the principal officers of the executive department or of such other body as Congress may by law provide, transmit within four days to the President pro tempore of the Senate and the Speaker of the House of Representatives their written declaration that the President is unable to discharge the powers and duties of his office. Thereupon Congress shall decide the issue, assembling within forty-eight hours for that purpose if not in session. If the Congress, within twenty-one days after receipt of the latter written declaration, or, if Congress is not in session, within twenty-one days after Congress is required to assemble, determines by two-thirds vote of both Houses that the President is unable to discharge the powers and duties of his office, the Vice President shall continue to discharge the same as Acting President; otherwise, the President shall resume the powers and duties of his office.

AMENDMENT XXVI [1971]   *(18-Year-Old Vote)*

Section 1. The right of citizens of the United States, who are eighteen years of age or older, to vote shall not be denied or abridged by the United States or by any State on account of age.

Section 2. The Congress shall have power to enforce this article by appropriate legislation.

AMENDMENT XXVII [1992]   *(Congressional Pay Raises)*

No law, varying the compensation for the services of the Senators and Representatives, shall take effect, until an election of Representatives shall have intervened.